CAUGHT BY THE WIND

Caught by the Wind

Gerald J. Gargiulo

International Psychoanalytic Books (IPBooks)
New York • http://www.IPBooks.net

Caught by the Wind

Published by IPBooks, Queens, NY
Online at: www.IPBooks.net

Copyright © 2021 Gerald J. Gargiulo

All rights reserved. This book may not be reproduced, transmitted, or stored, in whole or in part by any means, including graphic, electronic, or mechanical without the express permission of the author and/or publisher, except in the case of brief quotations embodied in critical articles and reviews.

ISBN: 978-1-949093-83-4

For Julia

Contents

Solitary 1
Awake 2
Hospitalized 3
Butterflies 4
Place Setting 5
Toscana in July* 6
Seasons 7
Silent Spells 9
Sunday Walks 10
Memory 12
Untitled 13
April Thoughts 14
Distraction 15
Last View 16
Passing 17
The Future from Behind 18
Encounter 20
Talking to Julia – 1 21
The Found World 22
Janus 23
Musings 24
On Reading Ammons 25
Recognition 26

Chartres	27
Surprise	28
Calvary	29
Undone	31
Reverie	32
Borderline Life	33
Uprooted	34
Sessions	35
Openings	36
Oxford Walks	37
Julia II	38
Late October	39
Acknowledgments	40
About the author:	41

In my experience poetry is as much about learning what one is thinking and experiencing as it is about writing. In the writing, we can touch our forgotten or left behind selves. For those who could not afford psychoanalysis, Freud recommended writing — freely. That is how many of these poems came to be, in that ongoing moment of remembering the past while creating the present.

I have spent my life walking with patients as we both tried to find a better path; individuals from whom I have benefitted deeply. But I have learned most from my life with my wife Julia, whose sensitivity and ever-present love infused my days with depth, joy and meaning.

The poems in this collection are, I hope, a testament to the beauty of life in all its shades.

SOLITARY

Are we not all
found by time

When lilacs fall
do we not grieve

Awake

Love is not confined
by thought

It is an open space
enlivening

Yearning
for equal view

Not time's child
but birthing hope

It lives outside
of wind and rain

Hospitalized

I was, for many years, an orphan
and when I found my father
he was dying.

A brief encounter
an accidental turn,
as we walked the corridors
chlorine swept with muted walls
when he,
no longer held by youth's injuries
sat for just a momentary pause,
and spoke the love
he could not speak before.

I have seen an oak tree fall
and still
I am very small.

Butterflies

Butterflies are more
than a yellow breeze
alighting arbitrarily
delicate, like love
so easily undone.

If you wave them away,
in a moment of forgetfulness,
your loss will be
an empty memory.

Place Setting

I live at the bottom
of an empty sea
full of microbes & other
forgotten things.

Tossed by unseen currents.

But your hold
grounds
and I feel the earth
as if it were
a returning friend.

Gift enough
at the bottom of a sea
getting on with life
getting on with love.

Toscana in July*

I have circled
Sienna stones
in measured pace
and wondered at the works of man
confining such a race.

Walked these gentle hills
and umbered streets
cobbling my hopes with images
forgot.

And like autumnal leaves'
repeated fall
I race
for memory's
recall.

---

*The Polio

Seasons

Spring is more than mild-flowered
sun-warmed wind
more than crocuses surprising us
with Sunday resurrections,
purpling a hill with promises.

There is an underleaf
forgotten,
stalking with surprises,
a hiding place
a lifetime walk,
back to childhood reverie –
on sand-piled seashores
hands in make-believe,
wondering who was more alone
sea, or self.

Forgotten,
as winter is
no season place
but ground to all that follows
quickening Spring
to life self-made.

In April,
no deciduous rebirth
but now,
by childhood memory
defined -
self-made, unmade,
remade.

Silent Spells

I am not a maple tree
Japanese in its delicacy.
Its leaf
five pointed
diminutive
is innocently green.

From my silence
could I grow that delicately?
Push out from the jumble of my roots
a sacred pointed leaf,
whose dance with the wind
is quite enough for it to be.

A water maple vigils nearby
enfolding like an ancient cathedral
the hard-won innocence
of the lighter green.
And I?
I am just a mirror
to the scene,
wondering who will catch the image next.

And what it is
that they will see.

Sunday Walks

I have often wondered, walking outside as I do
why, for such a stretch
the Earth lies flat
easy to the eye and foot.
Why does She rise, seemingly for no reason?
Sometime thirty, sometimes forty feet or more
strewn with rocks, which anyone can see
if they make the effort
to climb and enjoy the view.

How does Mother Earth decide -
I have always wondered -
to lie still
or sometimes to be noticed
as if to make a point,
a new perspective?
How does She do that?
Where and when
so simple, yet
so hidden.

Wouldn't it be better to just let things be?
Flat land is easy
not much to negotiate
not much to react to,
the view is straight and safe.
Why does She squeeze herself,
creating little mini mountains?
And yet She does.

Is it worth the effort?
The view?
I wish
She would tell me,
I need to know.

And quietly
She answered
sometimes I rise,
sometimes not.

Then
I understood.

Memory

Winter stretches time
carelessly
without regard for
what we need.

Spring,
forgiving and loving
as she is
knows the eye's yearning
and lights the way
in search of butterflies
and
other playful things.

Untitled

Love is more than the deed
more than the finding of a hand
in the night.

The seeds of life run deeper —

What haunts us more
memory or desire?

Or, are we flames
in a burning
we cannot know?

April Thoughts

Gentlest giant
had
by rain
laden
water maple
yesterday
I caught you
soberly framing
the non
      existent sky

Distraction

Spring slides from the corner of my eyes
into some forgotten, half empty space…

a memory,
      I have mused about
      a momentary pause
while waiting for the light to turn green
into an after flow of thoughts
just gone,
like incense hesitating
before its own forgetfulness.

I am jealous of the place,
of that breath of life
so yearned for,
yet so feared.

Last View

As waves rush in
in vengeance
or in love
they wash the flattened sand.

Patiently
a sea gull waits
the waves retreat
to dance,
and leave an etching
for a moment's
view.

I am waiting
too.

Passing

Winter rain washes
my dreams and hopes
memories and desires
it comes on sun-filled days
unbidden.

A quiet ocean's view
tells me you are gone.

This space of me
with it echoes
of life's residue
is no longer mine
with
Winter rain.

The Future from Behind

I have seen an eagle fall
and I concur
that death is near.

A mind
overcome with loss
no longer flies,
and I yearned
for butterflies,
who lean into the sky,
by six or seven I knew
that I could never fly.

How I regret the loss
of the oak leaf's fall.

When I was small
I thought I could dance the wind
a ballet too
by ten I knew,
why I had waited so.

II

Forty trees have I counted between the fence
and mirrored sea
what of me, asks the question,
what of me?

Sit me in a chair, and teach me
long ago
ah and oh
ah and oh.

III

I have heard an echo
as only children do,
bewildered with delight
when the world talks back to you.

I have heard an echo,
through season's pass
and I concur
I concur,
the Earth holds me still.

Encounter

Love is like a momentary wind
stirring up the fallen leaves
to dance
and find new lodging;
giving birth
to what we could not see
before.

Talking to Julia - 1

Can't I see your holding eyes,
just once more
sweetheart,
your smile that forgave the world
its
many injuries.

How can I remain standing without you?
You are me.
When you left, you took me with you
I know you didn't mean too
I know I would have done the same.

You left the world you loved
so carefully,
closed your eyes
to our blue and green earth.

I cannot hold your sadness at leaving.
How did you do that
so well?

The Found World

Past the midpoint of our lives
when wisdom's consolation interrupts
the rush of time
we recall, when first we
made the world
and knew it as our own.

But life betrays
by seasonal design
before each May
our absence grows,
compassion's shadow then brings
no relief.

Autumn tells
we are a memory of light
fleeing the forgetfulness
of night.

Janus

Spring light tells us
how to live –
while darkness holds
forgotten dreams.

Tossed by unknown winds,
men hold,
women enfold
and we are both
and we are none.

Spring light tells us
how to live
while darkness holds
forgotten dreams.

Musings

There is a narrow causeway
away from the safety
of the mainland;
sometimes
it floods and leaves no trace
no path,
no respite.

And if I hug you
and rise
like the sea,
will I be lost?
Or,
will you be there
with your boat
which I have longed
to rest in?

On Reading Ammons

It's not the leaving that it's about,
about leaving
there is no about.

It's about the silence
like a monotonously sleeping sea
quiet to the eyes
can we leave that way?

That way, nonexistence has
no argument with us.
We trouble it not,
disturbing with our memories
what cannot be disturbed.

No wonder we come again
again, to learn
it's not about the leaving
but leaving not troubled.

Not troubling the quiet
emptiness
which yearns to remember
us,
with no trouble at all.

Recognition

Are they tears,
that delicate touch of water
on early morning lawns?

I think there is sorrow…
no longer are the dreams of night
allowed,
even to the most innocent of greens
as they feel the space of day.

Chartres

Chartres
I am convinced
is so silent,
so still
because it holds,
as a grieving mother does,
the prayers of all those centuries.

Silent Lady of the plain
when I saw you
I knew
first view was but a memory
and I had come to tell you
I have lost a friend,

and forgotten
how to pray.

Surprise

Caught by the wind
we are leafing
together

While day sounds
hold us
aimlessly

Calvary

It was a calm Sunday morning
when mother called,
*Dad's blood pressure is dropping,
You should come.*

The Merritt south, familiar in its turns
and rolling views, was not new to me.
My wife and I silent,
memories, light traffic
were our allies.

Calvary Hospital understands
time.
It moves as quickly
as the anxiety in my eyes.

I sat beside him, both of us now
with slowed breathing.
His favored son, off at a meeting,
the son who was his mirror
was coming,
I was told.

And I was here
and I was then,
so many dreams and hopes
ago.

Quietly, I spoke
ignoring the coma,
It's okay, go now, its okay
I love you; I always have…

Over and over,
as if it was just
the two of us
in an empty world.

Warmth left his hand.
And I was flooded
with half a century
of tears.

Undone

Notice how the mind deceives the eye
walk a city street
talk of your last trip
while to the side of your desires
you see a sleeping man
with too much clothing
and no warmth.

Muse, if you can
was it a momentary slip?
Some unpaid bill,
some fight with the wife,
that went on too long?
Perhaps,
an inside rage,
the type we almost never recognize.

Then
the close out.
Too tired to play the game of
desires fulfilled.

Reverie

Could I undo a moment
or maybe two,
to upset the river's flow
   forgetful of its end

and have that moment
owned, untold
   to be forty,
again
with you

Borderline Life

When off my mind in
squared off space
nighttime shapes define
my soul
like winded leaves upon
the break
that dance a hundred ways.

There are no mirrors
in the place
the view alone cannot be held
I am the wall,
I am the space.

The shape
is what I have to straighten,
for just a length of time.

The wind rests
the leaves are mine.

Uprooted

The black top lady rides again
a memory of God's revenge
undone the sight of things unseen
the mirror and the view are all.

Night stars fill my mind with pain
yet the circle comes again.

Upon the cushion the lady mused
the whirlwinds of the days are gone.
I loved you for the things you said
it is life that leads us on.

I hear now in measured tones
yellow suns betraying souls.
I am had by things undone;
I miss the sound of children's fun
& the whisper of the breeze.

Don't enter here, where lilies lie
where graying eyebrows hid gray tears.
Death undoes the lie of years.

The blue guitar is long long gone
caught by the casting of the years.

Sessions

Try not to let your sadness
like rain drops on a morning lake
fall aimless and undo the work
so laboriously engaged
calling you by name.

Be twister, for a moment
even by the memory of brightly spaces and views
like seagull's flight,
bereft of purpose
except the row of currents
hidden from view.

Engage your
endangering space
the droplets of dark memory.
And like a bridge
recognize that other land,
that other April
as more the current of our dreams
and the lament
of our awareness.

Openings

I search for a space
where eagles nest
and spring winds visit.

New flights come
memory sleeps
   I begin.

Oxford Walks

Looking,
always looking
down at history
up…

Knowing
the stones hear us,
smell our presence,
the world forgets our words
but the walls remember,
quietly

Julia II

I am made
dumb with grief
my mind grows
weary.

When I look at Renoir
all I see is paint.

Only when I hear a waltz,
is death banished and we are dancing,
and all I want is to run away with you
and flee this thing,
the world calls death.

Somewhere,
we are still together,
laughing, caring
even fighting, a little.

But I am lost
and cannot find my way
Find me sweetheart
I need to hold you.

Late October

I hover over my loneliness
Leaves are sliding gently
Winter awaits my invite
    I decline.

Acknowledgments

Many of the poems in this collection have appeared in the text *Between Hours* (Salman Akhtar ed), in my text *Broken Fathers/Broken Sons*, (Wiley Publications) as well as in *The East Hampton Star: Seasons, Solitary, Toscana in July, Chartres, Silent Spells, On Reading Ammons, June Thoughts, Hospitalized, Butterflies.*

About the Author:

Gerald J. Gargiulo is a psychoanalyst, lecturer, and writer. He is the author of *Psyche, Self and Soul, Broken Fathers / Broken Sons*, and *Quantum Psychoanalysis*, and numerous professional articles in both academic and popular journals. He has lectured both in the United States as well as abroad. He is a former president of the Training Institute of the National Psychological Association for Psychoanalysis (NYC) as well as The International Forum for Psychoanalytic Education, and he presently serves on the editorial boards of *The Psychoanalytic Review*, *Psychoanalytic Psychology*, and *The International Journal of Applied Psychoanalytic Studies*.

Jerry loves gardening and seashores. He has two children and four grandchildren. His wife, Julia, passed away a number of years ago. She was a deeply devoted mother, an accomplished teacher, a therapist, and a much-loved individual by all who knew her.

www.ingramcontent.com/pod-product-compliance
Lightning Source LLC
Chambersburg PA
CBHW030202100526
44592CB00009B/401